The Romans

David Maule

Level 3

Series Editors: Andy Hopkins and Jocelyn Potter

Pearson Education Limited
Edinburgh Gate, Harlow,
Essex CM20 2JE, England
and Associated Companies throughout the world.

Pack ISBN: 978-1-4058-5214-2
Book ISBN: 978-1-4058-5071-1
CD-ROM ISBN: 978-1-4058-5072-8

This edition first published by Pearson Education Ltd 2007

1 3 5 7 9 10 8 6 4 2

Text copyright © David Maule 2007
Illustrations by Marcelo Sosa
Set in 11/13pt A. Garamond
Printed in China
SWTC/01
Produced for the Publishers by AC Estudio Editorial S.L.

All rights reserved; no part of this publication may be reproduced, stored in a retrieval system, or transmitted in any form or by any means, electronic, mechanical, photocopying, recording or otherwise, without the prior written permission of the Publishers.

Published by Pearson Education Ltd in association with Penguin Books Ltd, both companies being subsidiaries of Pearson Plc

Acknowledgements

The Publishers would like to thank Dr Peter Stewart, Senior Lecturer in Classical Art and its Heritage at the Courtauld Institute of Art, London, for reviewing the manuscript and providing comments and suggestions during the development of *The Romans*.

We are grateful to the following for permission to reproduce photographs:
Bridgeman Art Library: page 29 (Pollice Verso, 1872 oil on canvas), Gerome, Jean Leon (1824–1904) (© Phoenix Art Museum, Arizona, USA), page 32 (Death of Julius Caesar 100–44 BC oil on canvas), Camuccini, Vincenzo (1773–1844) (Museo e Gallerie Nazionali di Capodimonte, Naples, Italy); **Britain On View**: page 37; **Corbis**: page 4 (Bettman), page 6 (Vanni Archive), page 57 (bl) (© Gianni Giansanti / Immaginazione); **Getty Images**: iv (a) (Taxi/HH), (b) (Robert Harding World Imagery / Ruth Tomlinson), page 25 (Stone), page 33 (both) (Bridgeman Art Library), page 34 (Hulton Archive), page 43 (Robert Harding World Imagery / John Miller), page 47 (Bridgeman Art Library), page 49 (Roger Viollet / LL), page 55 (Riser / David Madison), page 57 (tr) (Photonica / C. Stevenson), (m) (Dorling Kindersley / Andy Crawford), (bm) (Stone / Jason Hawkes), (br) (Photographers Choice / Richard Elliott); **PunchStock Royalty Free Images:** page 39 (Photodisc), page 57 (tl) (Medioimages), (tm) (PhotoAlto)
Picture research by Natasha Jones / Lisa Wren

Every effort has been made to trace the copyright holders and we apologise in advance for any unintentional omissions. We would be pleased to insert the appropriate acknowledgement in any subsequent edition of this publication.

For a complete list of the titles available in the Penguin Active Reading series please write to your local Pearson Longman office or to: Penguin Readers Marketing Department, Pearson Education, Edinburgh Gate, Harlow, Essex CM20 2JE, England.

Contents

	Activities 1	iv
Chapter 1	The Roman Empire	1
Chapter 2	Life in Rome	4
	Activities 2	8
Chapter 3	The People of Rome: Rich and Poor	10
Chapter 4	The People of Rome: Slaves	13
	Activities 3	16
Chapter 5	The Wars with Carthage	18
Chapter 6	The Roman Army	21
	Activities 4	24
Chapter 7	Sport and Games	26
Chapter 8	Republic to Empire	31
	Activities 5	36
Chapter 9	Roads and Water	38
Chapter 10	Writing, Counting and Building	41
	Activities 6	44
Chapter 11	The Early Emperors	46
Chapter 12	The Empire and After	51
	Talk about it	56
	Write about it	57
	Project: A Roman Dinner Party	58

Activities 1

1.1 What's the book about?

How much do you know about Rome and the Romans?

1. Which of these modern countries was not part of the Roman Empire?
    a Denmark b Egypt c Turkey
2. When was the Roman empire at its largest?
    a 900 years ago b 1,900 years ago
    c 2,900 years ago
3. Which river runs through the city of Rome?
    a the Thames b the Danube c the Tiber
4. Which of these Roman emperors was not murdered?
    a Claudius b Caligula c Nero
5. What was the building in picture A for?
    a government b shopping c sport
6. What did the building in picture B carry?
    a water b horses c soldiers
7. Which of these rulers of Rome was a lover of the Egyptian queen Cleopatra?
    a Mark Antony b Brutus c Cassius
8. Who was Spartacus?
    a a Roman emperor b a Roman general c a slave
9. What is the Roman number IX?
    a nine b ten c eleven
10. Which of these men helped to destroy the Roman empire?
    a Attila the Hun b Genghis Khan c Hannibal

A

B

1.2 What happens first?

Work with another student and discuss these questions. Make notes below.

1. Look at the map on page 2. Find Rome. Which modern countries were in the west, east, north and south of the empire at its largest?
2. What do you know about life in Rome at that time?

Notes

CHAPTER 1

The Roman Empire

For the first but not the last time, the Romans won because they fought harder. And they were more ready to die.

● The Roman world

In the north of England the Romans built a wall. It was started by the emperor Hadrian in 122 AD* and took more than ten years to finish. It was 120 kilometres long and six metres high in places. About every seven kilometres there was a strong **camp**. The wall crossed England from sea to sea and many parts of it are still there today.

In the east of Syria, near the River Euphrates, is the old city of Dura-Europos. The Romans arrived there in 165 AD. They took the city and made it a centre for their wars against the people to the east. And, of course, they built walls around it. Those walls are still there today too. The Romans stayed in Dura-Europos for almost a hundred years.

In Britain and in the Middle East the Romans went farther. They moved north of Hadrian's Wall into Scotland, and past Dura-Europos into Iraq. But the walls in England and the Syrian city show the real ends of the Roman **empire**. And from one to the other it is almost 4,000 kilometres.

In the north of Europe, the Romans held all the land south of the rivers Rhine and Danube. In north Africa, they **ruled** the coastal lands from Egypt to Algeria. Their empire went right round the Mediterranean. But in the years before the growth of the empire, Rome was like every other city in Italy – no bigger, no richer and no stronger. So who were the Romans? How did they live? How did their government work? How was this great empire built, and how was it lost? And what did the Romans leave behind in the countries they ruled?

In this book we will look at all these questions. We will meet some of the Roman emperors: the good and the bad. And we will look at the lives of ordinary Romans. We will find out how this city was able to rule so much of the world.

● The beginning

The Romans believed that their city started in 753 BC. In fact, the Latin people moved into the area hundreds of years earlier. Some of them made their homes on the seven hills near the River Tiber. This was a very good place to choose.

---

* AD/BC: years after/before Christ was born

camp /kæmp/ (n) a place where people stay in tents for a short time
empire /ˈempaɪə/ (n) a group of countries that are under one government or *emperor*
rule /ruːl/ (v/n) to be the government of a country

1

The Roman Empire at its largest in 106 AD

There was an island in the river, so the river was easier to cross than in other parts. It was also 25 kilometres from Rome to the sea, so the city was safe from attack by foreign ships. But Roman ships could sail down the river to the sea and carry things to other places. People made money and the city began to grow.

In later years, its position became important for other reasons. Rome was in the centre of Italy, so it could attack to the north and the south. And Italy was a safe country. It had sea on three sides and mountains to the north. It was also in the centre of the Mediterranean. When the Romans began to attack other countries, they attacked from a good position.

In the early years of Rome, the Greeks were building cities in the south of Italy. From them the Romans learned many skills, like reading and writing. To the north were the Etruscans. These people had many Greek ideas and some of their own. From them the Romans learned a lot about building.

The Romans believed that two brothers, Romulus and Remus, started their city. Then Romulus killed Remus and became the first king of Rome. After Romulus, Rome was ruled by six more kings. None of these was the son of the last king. After a king died, the people chose the next one. From the start, ordinary people were part of the government of Rome. The last king was Tarquinius Superbus ('Tarquin the Proud'). In about 509 BC the Romans

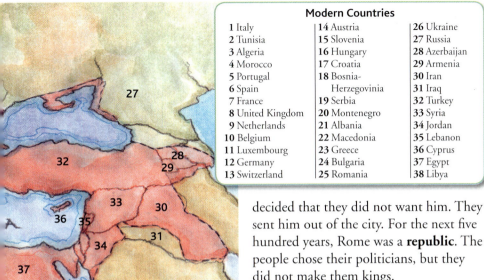

Modern Countries		
1 Italy	14 Austria	26 Ukraine
2 Tunisia	15 Slovenia	27 Russia
3 Algeria	16 Hungary	28 Azerbaijan
4 Morocco	17 Croatia	29 Armenia
5 Portugal	18 Bosnia-Herzegovinia	30 Iran
6 Spain	19 Serbia	31 Iraq
7 France	20 Montenegro	32 Turkey
8 United Kingdom	21 Albania	33 Syria
9 Netherlands	22 Macedonia	34 Jordan
10 Belgium	23 Greece	35 Lebanon
11 Luxembourg	24 Bulgaria	36 Cyprus
12 Germany	25 Romania	37 Egypt
13 Switzerland		38 Libya

decided that they did not want him. They sent him out of the city. For the next five hundred years, Rome was a **republic**. The people chose their politicians, but they did not make them kings.

After Romulus, Rome grew slowly stronger. In 430 BC there were disagreements with the city's nearest neighbour, the rich Etruscan city of Veii, 20 kilometres to the north, on the other side of the Tiber. The two cities wanted the same river crossings and the same land. Over the next forty years they were at war many times. The wars finally ended when the ruler of Rome, Camillus, ordered the Romans to fight all year. Before that they were able to go back to their farms every year. For the first but not the last time, the Romans won because they fought harder. And they were more ready to die.

For the next two hundred years Rome was at war with its neighbours in Italy. At first the Romans fought with the other cities around it. When these cities were **defeated**, they came under Roman rule. Some of them began to work closely with Rome. Their people could become **citizens** but could not choose the politicians. Other cities were not as friendly with Rome, but they understood its importance. Rome was a dangerous enemy. Later, as its **army** grew bigger, Rome went to war with neighbouring peoples. By 272 BC it ruled all of Italy south of a line from Pisa to Rimini. Then Rome looked towards new lands in the north, and also across the sea.

republic /rɪˈpʌblɪk/ (n) a country where people choose the politicians. A republic has no king or emperor.
defeat /dɪˈfiːt/ (v/n) to win a war against someone
citizen /ˈsɪtəzən/ (n) a free person in a country who is protected by the law
army /ˈɑːmi/ (n) a large number of soldiers who belong to one state

CHAPTER 2

Life in Rome

Life for the rich and the poor was very different, but they often enjoyed the same things. Almost everyone went to the baths because most baths were free.

● Arriving in Rome

It is 165 AD. Marcus Aurelius is emperor. Hadrian's Wall is thirty years old, and the army has just taken Dura-Europos. Rome is the strongest and largest city in the world – and you are walking towards it. As you follow the Appian Way, from the south, you see the smoke first. It comes from the work places and houses of one million people.

As you get nearer, still outside the city walls, you walk past the entrances to rich people's houses and past the resting places of the dead. Then, at last, in front of you, the real city begins. You walk through the Appian Gate.

Entering Rome in the Appian Way

4

This is the highest building that you have ever seen. As you pass through, you can see the tops of even larger buildings. All around you there are people. Some are buying and selling. Some are eating in the street. They are living and dying in front of you.

The buildings are close to the street. Windows are open and people talk. Here and there, between the newer buildings, are very old ones. The Romans like old religious buildings. Men are working in the empty space where a building has burned down. Already, they are clearing the ground for a new building. Land is expensive in Rome and empty space is filled very quickly.

There is no other place in the world like this. This is Rome.

● Houses

For most of the poorer people of Rome, home was one room in a high building. As time passed, there was very little space in the city and people built higher and higher. In the end, the government had to pass a law: buildings could have no more than five floors. But some owners did not worry about that. Sometimes buildings fell down, or they caught fire. When this happened, a rich man sometimes bought the land cheaply. Then he put up another building. And sometimes an owner started a fire in a building because he wanted to put up a bigger one in its place.

● Daily Life

Romans usually lived their lives in the daytime. They got up with the sun and most people went to bed early. People did not usually go out in the evening because the streets were not safe. There were no police. When there was trouble, the government sometimes used soldiers, but not often. They were nervous about soldiers in the city. When rich people went out to dinner at night, they took **slaves** with them. Poorer people did not give dinner parties. They usually met their friends at the baths in the afternoon, and then they went home.

There were shops on every street in Rome. These were often on the ground floor of the buildings where people lived. People also sold from tables in the streets. The government tried to stop this, but people took little notice of the laws. The biggest shopping centre was Trajan's Market, built in about 110 AD. There were five floors of shops, and tables outside for people to buy things from. You could buy food, oil and wine there.

Rome was very noisy because it produced so much. There were places of work across the city. Often the workers sold in their own shops the things that

---

slave /sleɪv/ (n) someone who is owned by another person. He or she has to work, usually without pay. The use of *slaves* is *slavery*.

The Romans

Rome in the time of Constantine (306–337 AD)

they produced. And every nine days there were markets. People came from the country to sell food from their farms. At the same time, they bought things made in the city.

● **A visit to the baths**

Life for the rich and the poor was very different, but they often enjoyed the same things. Almost everyone went to the baths because most baths were free. Romans liked to keep their bodies clean, so most people visited the baths once a day.

There were three very large baths in Rome. The biggest of all were the Baths of Diocletian in the north-east of the city. Opened in 306 AD, they were more than 300 metres long on each side. They could hold thousands of

aqueduct /ˈækwɪdʌkt/ (n) something that carries water through rock and across valleys to towns and cities

Chapter 2 – Life in Rome

customers at a time. The Baths of Trajan were near the Colosseum and the Baths of Caracalla were near the Appian Gate. These large baths used a lot of water and each had its own **aqueduct**. There were also hundreds of smaller, local baths. By 300 AD there were more than eight hundred and fifty baths in the city.

When you arrived at the baths, you changed your clothes. You put on simple shoes and did some exercise. You could lift weights, run, practise fighting or play ball games. After this you went into a hot room which was kept at about 40°C. You took a hot bath and slaves cleaned you with oil – the Romans did not use soap. The next room was colder. You sat there for some time while your body temperature fell. There was a pool of cold water in the room. You could jump into it. After this you could go for a swim in the open air pool.

The baths were not just for washing and exercise. The larger ones had beautiful gardens. Romans liked to walk in these and talk to their friends or just think. There were also libraries, religious buildings, meeting rooms and shops. Some people spent a large part of their lives at the baths.

Most Roman towns across the empire had free baths, and rich families also had their own private baths. In some towns, hot water came up naturally from under the ground. In some, the water was good for people's health. This was true of the city of Bath in England, and the Roman baths are still there now. In later years, the Roman empire was cut into two parts, east and west. Constantinople, now Istanbul, became capital of the Eastern Empire. Many baths were built there, and Turkish baths today are very similar.

Activities 2

2.1 Were you right?

Look back at your answers to Activity 1.2 on page iv. Then tick (✓) the statements about the city of Rome that are correct.

1. [✓] Rome was a crowded city.
2. [ ] The air was clean.
3. [ ] Land was cheap.
4. [ ] Buildings were never more than two floors.
5. [ ] Many people were afraid to go out at night.
6. [ ] There were shops and markets.
7. [ ] Romans didn't often wash.

2.2 What more did you learn?

Who were the people in *italics*? Write the letters, A–H.

> A Diocletian   B Hadrian   C Marcus Aurelius   D Romulus
> E Tarquin   F The Etruscans   G The Greeks   H Trajan

1. [B] *He* built a wall across the north of England.
2. [ ] *They* built cities in the south of Italy.
3. [ ] *They* lived to the north of Rome.
4. [ ] The Romans believed *he* started their city.
5. [ ] *He* was the last king of Rome.
6. [ ] *He* was emperor in 165 AD.
7. [ ] *He* built a market in Rome.
8. [ ] *He* built baths in the north-east of Rome.

The Romans

2.3 Language in use

Look at the sentence on the right. Then write a sentence about each picture. What have these people just done?

> The army **has just taken** Dura-Europos.

....
....
....

....
....
....

2.4 What's next?

Look at the picture of a large Roman house on page 11. In what ways is it similar to and different from a modern house in your country? Make notes.

Notes

CHAPTER 3

The People of Rome: Rich and Poor

The head of the house was the oldest man. He was in a very strong position and he made all the decisions about people in the house.

● The classes

Through the history of Rome, a small group of families formed the upper class. In the early days they ruled the city, but slowly the lower class became stronger. As time passed, a middle class grew out of the lower classes. They did not rule like the upper class but they had a lot of money. By 287 BC each class had its own politicians. These were some of the 300 men in the Senate, the most important part of the government of Rome.

● Citizens

At first, all citizens of Rome had to live in the city. Later, people near the city were able to become citizens. In time, this became possible for people across the empire. But only free men could be citizens. Women and slaves could not. Citizens in the city of Rome could vote for Roman politicians, but other people could not. Citizens could also join the **legions**. They could make business or marriage agreements with the protection of the law. They could join the Senate as senators. They could take another person to the law courts. And if they broke the law, they could be taken to court. A citizen could not be put in prison, punished or killed without a court judgment. And when a citizen was killed, this was done quickly. Many other criminals and enemies of Rome were hung on crosses. They were left there to die a slow and painful death.

If you were not born a citizen, you could become one in three ways. First, you could join the army, not in one of the legions but as a soldier on lower pay. After twenty-five years, you became a citizen, and your children did too. Second, you could pay a large amount of money. Third, you could be freed by your owner and become a citizen.

Everybody wanted to be a Roman citizen, and this held the empire together.

● The homes of the rich

There was one big difference between the homes of rich Romans and most houses today. Modern houses usually have a lot of windows. People live in the house and look out. But the houses of rich Romans looked in. There were few

---

legion /ˈliːdʒən/ (n) a group of about 5,000 Roman soldiers. These soldiers were called *legionaries*.

windows onto the street, except small ones on upper floors. In fact, the buildings did not really look like houses from the outside because there were shops along the walls. The owner of the building earned money from the shops, and the shops kept the house away from the noise and smell of the streets. The best parts of a Roman house were inside. A strong house, with only a few small windows, was also good protection against criminals.

There was one more reason for the small windows. The Romans did not use much glass. They could make window glass, but only in small sizes. Also, the glass was not completely clear and let very little light through. Glass was mainly used in the baths.

The house of a rich Roman family

Roman houses were built round open squares, so light and fresh air could pass into the house. But houses could also be cold in winter, so in colder parts of the empire the main rooms were heated by hot air under the floors.

Many people lived in the house. Unmarried uncles and aunts and other relatives often lived with the family. Sometimes guests stayed for a long time. Houses also had slaves, so there were rooms – sometimes underground – for them. Most slaves in private houses were women, and they shopped, cooked, cleaned, washed clothes and sheets, looked after the kitchen garden and carried water. All these jobs were much harder at that time than they are today.

The head of the house was the oldest man. He made all the decisions about the people who lived there. He could punish or kill his slaves, his workers, and even his own grown-up children. He could make and end marriages. And, like all men, he could end his own marriage. In Rome this was very simple; a man had only to say a few words to his wife.

The owner's wife was also important. She kept the keys to the doors and the money boxes. Every day she told the slaves and servants what to do. She also looked after the children. The home was important to women because they did not go out often. Shopping was usually done by slaves.

CHAPTER 4

The People of Rome: Slaves

Six thousand were taken alive. They were hung up on wooden crosses along the Appian Way, the first Roman road.

● Prisoners of war

Most slaves were prisoners of war. They were enemy soldiers but their wives and children were taken too. Sometimes, all the people in a town were sold as slaves. Businessmen travelled with the army and bought prisoners from the Roman soldiers. In the early days, slaves were sold one after another in a market. But as time passed, the number of prisoners grew. They were sold by the hundred, then by the thousand and even the hundred thousand.

At first, only the richest families had slaves, but slaves became cheaper and cheaper. In time, most house owners had a few. Rich people owned hundreds and the emperor owned thousands.

● Work

Slaves did many different types of work. If they were from the east of the empire, they were often used in the home. They worked as teachers, water carriers,

House slaves

readers, secretaries, doormen, doctors, waiters, musicians and gardeners. House slaves had the easiest lives. Often they were the children of slave parents and grew up as part of the family. These slaves spoke the same language as their owners. Guests judged an owner by how they looked. Slaves lived in their own part of the house, but those rooms were not always bad. The writer Pliny the Younger wrote that he was able to use his slaves' rooms as guestrooms.

Most house slaves were paid something for their work. Because of this, they wanted to live quietly and save money. Then, one day, they could live as free men and women. Many of them were given permission to marry. This was good for the owner, because their children became slaves too. Slaves could also learn to read and write or to do skilled work.

Slaves from countries to the north usually did harder work. They built roads, bridges and houses. Some were sent to work on farms. We think of Romans as city people but many more citizens lived in the country than in the city. Also, rich people usually had land and a house in the country where they tried to spend their summers. Their farms were quite large and had a lot of slaves. The slaves did the heavy work and also made tools and equipment for farming or for the house. Because they were not so close to the family, the lives of farm slaves were more unpleasant.

Perhaps the worst place for a slave to work was underground. The Romans used thousands of slaves to find gold and other metals. A Greek, Diodorus, described life underground. He wrote that the air was very bad. Fires were lit to break the rocks. These fires took all the air and made the place very hot. Also, hot rocks sometimes let out dangerous gases. Slaves often died painful deaths.

The slaves broke the rock into smaller pieces. They often had to lie on their backs or their sides to do the work. Sometimes pieces of rock broke off and fell into their eyes, or the roof fell and killed them. If they did not die underground, sooner or later they died of too much work. This was the real cost of the gold for the rings and cups of rich Romans.

● Slave wars

Slaves sometimes escaped or killed their owners, but three times, large numbers of slaves went to war with Rome. The first two wars were in Sicily. The third war was started by a slave called Spartacus in 73 BC. 120,000 slaves joined him and they defeated Roman armies a number of times. In the end the Senate had to send ten legions against the slaves. Six thousand were taken alive. They were hung up on wooden crosses along the Appian Way, the first Roman road. They died terrible deaths.

Chapter 4 – The People of Rome: Slaves

● **Better lives for slaves**

Many slaves were able to save money. Then they could buy their **freedom**. Others were freed by their owners after years of good work. Freed slaves often opened small shops – and, after some time, some owned large businesses. Most house slaves were freed at about the age of thirty. They could then do useful work and make money. In fact, they often became customers of the owner, and helped him to make more money. Slaves were also often freed when their owner died.

As time passed, the lives of slaves became easier. The emperor Claudius (41–54 AD) passed a new law. When a slave owner sent an old or sick slave away from his house, the slave became free. Under the next emperor, Nero, slaves could take their owners to court. Some time after that, slaves were able to ask for their freedom if they had a bad owner. Also, when an owner killed his slave without a good reason, it became murder.

In the later empire, there were more changes to the law. By the year 300 AD, men could not sell their children as slaves. At one time, if you could not pay your bills, you became a slave. This also stopped. People's feelings about slavery changed too. The early Christians were not against slavery but they did not like unkindness towards slaves. But some people began to feel that slavery was wrong.

● **How slavery changed Rome**

Slavery was everywhere at that time, not only in the Roman empire. The Greeks had slaves in all their cities. Slavery was not against the law in European and North American countries until the 1800s. In fact, there are still slaves in some parts of the world today.

But slavery changed Rome. By 100 AD, one person in three in the city was a slave. Around the empire, it was about one person in five - about 12 million people. All the heavy work and a lot of the skilled work was done by slaves. Because of this, there was less work for free people in Rome. As slaves became cheaper, the problem got worse. Free food had to be given to a growing number of poor people, and this cost a lot of money. To keep the people happy, fights in the Colosseum and other **arenas** became bigger and more expensive.

---

freedom /ˈfriːdəm/ (n) the state of being *free*
arena /əˈriːnə/ (n) a large open space with seats around it, for games and fights

Activities 3

3.1 Were you right?

Look back at your answers to Activity 2.4. Then choose the best endings for each sentence.

1 Houses had few windows because … ☐ ☐
2 There were shops along the outside walls because … ☐ ☐
3 Houses were built around open squares because … ☐

> a people liked light and fresh air in the house.
> b they kept the house away from the noisy, smelly streets.
> c Rome was a dangerous place.
> d the owner of the building earned money from them.
> e Roman glass only came in small sizes.

3.2 What more did you learn?

Answer the questions.

1 What job did people do in the Senate?
   They were politicians

2 What job did men do if they joined a legion?

3 Who were protected by the law courts?

4 What happened to prisoners of war?

5 Why were Romans happy when their slaves married?

6 Who started the third slave war against the Romans?

7 How did the army of slaves die on the Appian Way?

8 Why was the use of slaves a problem for poor Romans?

3.3 Language in use

Look at the sentence on the right. Then complete the questions with another form of the word in *italics*.

> They could make business or marriage **agreements** with the **protection** of the law.

1 How were slaves ..... *punished* .....?
   For many, the *punishment* was death.
2 How were Roman houses .... from ours today?
   One big *difference* was the number of windows.
3 Who .... if his slave should die?
   It was the *decision* of the oldest man in the house.
4 Why did businessmen .... with the army?
   They bought slaves on their *travels*.
5 Was death .... for workers underground?
   Yes, the workers often died in great *pain*.
6 How did a slave become ....?
   Many could buy their *freedom*.

3.4 What's next?

Look at the pictures and discuss the questions. Then write your answers.

1 For some time, the Romans put bridges on their ships. Later, they stopped using them.

a Why were the bridges useful?
....
....

b What was the problem with them?
....
....

2 When the people of Carthage were attacked, they moved inside the city walls. The Romans won in the end. Why, do you think?
....
....

CHAPTER 5

The Wars with Carthage

Hannibal got through to Italy, but with only 26,000 men and three elephants. The rest lay dead in the snow.

● The first war

Carthage was in modern Tunisia, just outside Tunis. Its people travelled a long way by ship, buying and selling. By 300 BC the Carthaginians **occupied** the coastal lands of north Africa, the islands of Corsica and Sardinia, the west of Sicily and the south of Spain.

The Carthaginians were good sailors, but most of their soldiers came from other places. These soldiers were paid for their work – if the Carthaginians had enough money. The Carthaginians were businessmen. For them, money was very important. Their politicians paid for their jobs, and little was done without payment.

The Romans were different in many ways. They chose their own politicians and they did not have a high opinion of businessmen. Their legionaries were Roman citizens. But the Romans had no warships. They knew very little about sailing and nothing about fighting at sea.

In 264 BC a small private army, the Mamertines, took the Sicilian city of Messina, across the water from Italy. Carthage sent its army to help them. The Romans were not happy that a Carthaginian army was so close. So 40,000 men crossed into Sicily. They took Messina and some other towns, but Sicily is a hilly country and the Roman army could not move around easily. The Romans started to build ships.

At that time, warships were built with a long, sharp piece of wood at the front. They sailed into an enemy ship and tried to make a hole in it. But the Romans knew more about land war than fighting at sea, so they put a wooden bridge on the front of each ship. It stood on one of its ends and then dropped onto the enemy ship. The Romans were than able to cross the bridge and fight in the same way as on land. The ships from the two empires met off the coast of Sicily in 260 BC. The new way of fighting surprised the Carthaginians and the Romans won.

But the heavy bridges made the Roman ships unsafe. As the war continued, many ships were destroyed by storms and the Romans stopped using the bridges.

The Romans still wanted to fight the Carthaginians on land, so they sent an army to north Africa. This time the Carthaginians defeated them. Another army

occupy /ˈɒkjʊpaɪ/ (v) to take soldiers into a place and make the place part of your state

Roman warships

went to help, but their ships were destroyed in a storm. With difficulty, the Romans found money to build more ships. In 241 BC they defeated the Carthaginian ships near the west coast of Sicily. Carthage finally stopped fighting and Sicily became part of the Roman empire.

● **The second war**

After the first war, the Carthaginians had to pay a large amount of money to Rome every year. To get the money, they took more and more of the south of Spain. In 219 BC the Carthaginian **general** Hannibal attacked the Spanish city of Sagunto. This was under Roman protection, so Rome went to war again.

Hannibal moved his army north through Spain and east towards Italy. He wanted to cross the Alps before winter started. He had 38,000 foot soldiers and 8,000 horsemen. He also took thirty-seven war **elephants**. As the Carthaginians climbed into the Alps, they were attacked by local people. The weather also got worse. Hannibal got through to Italy, but with only 26,000 men and three elephants. The rest lay dead in the snow.

The Carthaginian general moved south and defeated two Roman armies. But Hannibal did not try to take Rome. He continued to the south of Italy and

---

general /ˈdʒenərəl/ (n) an important officer in the army
elephant /ˈeləfənt/ (n) a very large grey animal with big ears and a long nose

The Romans

Hannibal's army in the Alps

looked for help from the cities there. Another Roman army followed Hannibal but did not attack. In 216 BC, at Cannae, Hannibal turned and destroyed them.

Rome then sent an army to north Africa and moved towards Carthage. Hannibal was called home to defend the city. The two armies met at Zama near Carthage in 202 BC and this time the Romans won. They destroyed the walls of the city, and left the Carthaginians with only ten ships. Hannibal escaped, but in the end he killed himself.

● **The third war**

Massinissa was the king of Numidia, in modern Algeria. In 151 BC he attacked Carthage from the south. Massinissa was a friend of Rome, so the Romans went to war with Carthage again.

The Carthaginians built stronger city walls and moved inside them. For three years the Romans attacked. The Carthaginians fought well, but in the end they had no food left and the Romans broke through the walls. Thousands of people died in six days of street fighting and the rest were sold into slavery. Then the Romans completely destroyed Carthage. They knocked down the walls and the buildings and nobody was able to live there. Years later, a new Roman town was built in its place.

At the end of more than a hundred years of war with Carthage, Rome ruled Corsica, Sardinia, Sicily, the south of Spain and north Africa. In the time between the second and third wars, the Romans went to war with Philip V of Macedonia. Philip was friendly with Carthage and he also ruled most of Greece. The Romans fought three wars against him and by 168 BC they occupied all of Macedonia and Greece. Rome was becoming a world empire.

CHAPTER 6

The Roman Army

Because Marius was successful, the people made him a ruler of Rome again. After that, nobody ruled Rome without an army behind him.

● The early Roman army

In the early days of Rome, people had to own a house in the city or a farm if they wanted to be a soldier. They also needed money to buy their own equipment.

The men fought in three lines. At first, the richer men, with better equipment, stood in the back line. As time passed, there were changes. The soldiers still fought in three lines, but now the youngest men stood in the front line. Behind them were men in their twenties and thirties and the older men were at the back.

But the three lines still did not work very well. Roman soldiers were defeated a number of times, and in 110 BC, in the north of Algeria, King Jugurtha destroyed a Roman army. A new man, Gaius Marius, became the Roman general in Africa.

● Marius

Marius brought poor men into the army. Many joined and he was successful in Africa. Then, in France, two Roman armies were destroyed and 80,000 men died. Marius was again asked to be general. This time he worked for three years and completely changed the army. The men were put together in groups of eighty. Six of these groups fought side by side and sixty of them became a legion.

Roman soldiers

The legionaries wore heavy armour to protect their bodies. They carried a javelin, a sword, a knife and a shield. The swords were short, only 60 centimetres long. Javelins were two metres long. They were thick pieces of wood with thin metal at the end which came to a sharp point. The legionaries threw them at the enemy and a javelin could go right through a shield.

A legion also had 120 soldiers on horses. They rode in front to search for the enemy. They also carried messages. Other men did special work. They looked after the horses, the swords and equipment. Doctors looked after the men, and they were very good at it. In fact, medicine in the Roman army was better than in any European army until the late 1800s. Because of the doctors, the soldiers drank clean water and built good toilets. Roman soldiers were usually healthy and very few died from illness.

This new army was very successful. Marius' legions defeated the Cimbri, a German people, in the north of Italy. In 90 BC people in other parts of Italy were able to become citizens, and many of them joined the legions. Rome also used soldiers who were not citizens. These men could not join the legions. They had lighter equipment. They usually stood at the front and attacked the enemy first. After twenty-five years in the army, these men could become citizens.

● Behind walls

When a Roman legion got close, its enemies often looked for the protection of a strong camp, behind high walls. The Romans then attacked under the wall, through it or over it. They made holes in the ground. They knocked the walls down. They built up earth until it reached the top of the walls. Sometimes the soldiers stood close together and held their shields over their heads. Then other men climbed up onto the shields and crossed the wall. The Romans also used different types of machine that threw large stones at the defenders. None of the machines were Roman ideas. They came from the Greeks, but the Romans made changes to them and the machines worked better.

● Army life

When a legion was moving from place to place, the soldiers built a camp every night. Near the end of the day, they found a good place to stop, with fresh water and grass. They put sticks in the ground at the corners and along each side. Then the soldiers made a long hole in the ground around the outside of the camp. They threw the earth up into a wall. There were no gates, but another wall was built a few metres in front of the entrance. After this, the men put up their tents and cooked their evening meal. Then some stayed awake while the others slept. In the morning, they moved to a new place and built a new camp.

When a legion stayed in one place for a longer time, they built a stronger camp. Many of these camps can still be seen today. Towns grew up outside them, and the soldiers' women lived there. Until about 200 AD the men could not get married; the army probably did not want to pay money to a dead soldier's wife. But a soldier's woman got his money when he died. And their sons became citizens if they joined the legion.

● Soldiers and politicians

Marius was a successful general, so he also became an important politician. After that, nobody ruled Rome without an army behind him. Soldiers stayed with the same legion for years. Many never saw Rome. Each ruler of Rome had his own legions. When there was trouble between politicians, the legionaries, under their general, fought against other Romans. At some times, Romans fought against Romans almost as much as against foreign enemies.

One reason for this was the way the legions worked. Each group of eighty men had an officer who was a professional soldier. These men joined the army in the same way as every other man and became officers as a result of hard work. But above them were men from rich families. They were often younger and they did not stay with the army for a long time. They were there because high-class Romans also had to be successful soldiers. Many politicians used the army to become rulers.

The wars between Romans continued until Augustus became emperor in 27 BC.

A Roman legion camps for the night.

Activities 4

4.1 Were you right?

Look back at your answers to Activity 3.4. Then circle the best answer to these questions.

1 Why did the Romans start to build warships?
 a They were afraid of the Sicilians.
 b They wanted to attack the Carthaginians.
 c They preferred to fight at sea.

2 What happened at the end of the first war with the Carthaginians?
 a The Romans took Spain.
 b The Romans paid the Carthaginians.
 c The Romans took Sicily.

3 What happened at the end of the second war?
 a The Romans killed Hannibal.
 b The Romans destroyed the walls of Carthage.
 c The Romans were defeated.

4 Why did the Romans attack Carthage again?
 a The Romans were helping a friend.
 b The Carthaginians attacked Rome.
 c The Romans needed food.

4.2 What more did you learn?

Write the correct numbers.

| 3 | 10 | 37 | 200 | 4,800 | 8,000 |

1 ☐ The number of elephants that Hannibal took into the Alps.
2 ☐ The number of horsemen that Hannibal took into the Alps.
3 ☐ The number of ships that Carthage had after the second war.
4 ☐ The number of lines of soldiers in the early Roman army.
5 ☐ The number of soldiers in a legion.
6 ☐ The number of horsemen in a legion.
7 ☐ The number of years without war in the empire after Augustus.

The Romans

4.3 Language in use

Look at the sentence on the right. Then write questions for these answers.

> **To get** the money, they took more and more of the south of Spain.

1. Why did the Romans build warships?
   To take soldiers to Sicily.
2. ....
   To cross onto enemy ships.
3. ....
   To attack the Romans in Italy.
4. ....
   To protect the city from Roman attacks.
5. ....
   To occupy Macedonia and Greece.

4.4 What's next?

What do you think? Are these sentences about the Colosseum true (✓) or not (✗)?

1. ☐ People and animals fought there.
2. ☐ It could hold 100,000 people.
3. ☐ They could all leave in about 15 minutes.
4. ☐ It was the biggest arena in the Roman Empire.
5. ☐ It was sometimes filled with water for fights between ships.
6. ☐ It was sometimes covered to protect people from the sun.
7. ☐ In later times, lifts took people to the upper floors.
8. ☐ Sometimes the games lasted for days.

CHAPTER 7

Sport and Games

On a wall in the old city of Pompeii are the words 'Crescens the fighter holds the hearts of all the girls.'

● The Circus Maximus

When we think about sport and games in Rome, we probably think about the Colosseum. About half of this building is still standing. In Roman times it held about 50,000 people. **Gladiators** fought other gladiators there. Criminals and Christians were eaten by wild animals. But this building was not started until 72 AD, and the Colosseum was not the largest place for sport in Rome. The Circus Maximus was much bigger.

The Circus Maximus was built near the Palatine Hill and grew over the years. Emperors gave money to make it bigger and better. By 100 AD it could hold around 250,000 people, all with seats. Today, even the largest football grounds in the world only hold about 100,000 people.

At the Circus Maximus, you did not see fights between men, women and animals. You saw horses. The early Romans enjoyed horse races, but later people preferred **chariot** races. They became very popular, with their crashes and sudden deaths.

In fact, the Circus Maximus was not the only place for chariot racing in the city. At different times there were two other large arenas. The emperors Caligula and Nero built their own private arenas on the other side of the River Tiber, and there were many others across the empire.

Rich Romans liked to pay for chariot races. It made their names well-known and it kept the people happy. The Roman writer Juvenal said, 'The people are not interested in politicians now. They only want bread and chariot races.'

Very little of the Circus Maximus is still there today. Most of its stones were taken away and used in later buildings. Now there is only a large empty space in the centre of Rome. But we know its shape and its size. We can also imagine what it looked like. There is a similar arena in Libya. The Circus Maximus was not like a modern sports ground because it was straight across one end. There were twelve gates where the chariots came in together. Across the centre line was a wall. The chariots drove around this.

---

gladiator /ˈglædieɪtə/ (n) a man who fought animals or other men
chariot /ˈtʃærɪət/ (n) a vehicle with two wheels that is pulled by horses. It was used in war and for races.

A chariot race at the Circus Maximus

● The races

Chariot teams in Rome at that time were like football teams today. People followed their favourite. From the time of Augustus (27 BC–14 AD), there were four big teams in Rome. They took their names from their colours – the blues, the greens, the reds and the whites. The blues and the greens were the most popular. When chariot teams lost races, their followers sometimes started trouble, just like troublemakers in football today.

There were usually four chariots in a race, and people put money on their favourites. Sometimes the chariots were pulled by two horses, but four were more usual. For each race they went seven times around the arena. The drivers fought to get to the inside. But they had to be careful not to crash into a corner.

Some drivers started at the age of thirteen. Like the gladiators in the Colosseum, they were usually slaves. It was a dangerous job but a few lived. They became rich and famous – and free men. The best drivers were as popular as football stars today. The Roman writer Martial once said, 'Chariot drivers and their horses are famous, but nobody knows the names of writers.'

The most famous driver of all, Diocles, stopped racing in 150 AD at the age of forty-two after 3,000 wins. But few drivers had time to enjoy their money. Scorpus won 200 races. He was rich when he died in a crash at the age of twenty-seven. Most died when they were young and poor. Perhaps only the owners of the teams were the real winners.

● The Colosseum

In the very early days of Rome, a rich man's slaves were killed when he died. Later, pairs of slaves were given swords and had to fight to the death. Prisoners of war were killed in the same way, but sometimes the winner was given his freedom. Often, these fighters became gladiators, and they fought in arenas all over the empire. The largest and best known of these arenas was the Colosseum.

When the emperor Nero died in 68 AD, he left a palace with large gardens and a private lake. Four years later the emperor Vespasian emptied the lake and started to build the Colosseum. He died before the work was completed. It was finished by his son Titus when he became emperor.

The fighting area was 83 metres long and 48 metres wide. It was built of stone, with sand on top. The stones were above underground rooms for the gladiators and the animals. The seats at the front were taken by the emperor, politicians and other important people. The higher seats were for ordinary Romans. All the seats had numbers. There were five floors, and the top of the building was 48 metres high. By the year 300 AD the Colosseum even had lifts, for taking animals up to the fighting area.

There were seats for about 45,000 people, with room for perhaps another 5,000 standing. There were seventy-six numbered entrances so the crowd could leave quickly – in about fifteen minutes. Not many modern football grounds can empty in this time. At the top of the building, long pieces of wood held a cloth cover. On hot days this cover was pulled across to protect people from the sun. The fighting area was sometimes filled with water and then there were fights between ships.

● Gladiators

Most gladiators were slaves, and most of these were prisoners of war. There were also criminals, some poor men, and a few upper-class men who needed the money. Women fought as gladiators, too, until this was stopped in 200 AD. Too many women wanted to do it.

The learners were kept in small stone rooms in gladiator schools. They could only leave the rooms to practise. They fought with wooden swords and javelins at first. After this, the real, heavier equipment was easier to use.

There were different types of gladiator, but they all carried a shield and wore armour on their arms or legs. The important parts of their bodies – their chests, for example – were not covered. One type of gladiator only fought wild animals. Some men fought on foot and some on horses, sometimes to the death.

Life as a gladiator could end very suddenly, but it was not all bad. Gladiators only fought about three times a year. After their lives as fighters began, they were not locked up. Some lived in their own houses.

On the night before the games, there was a big dinner for the gladiators. Some Roman women liked to go to these. The writer Juvenal tells us about a politician's wife called Eppia. She enjoyed the dinners and ran off to Egypt with a gladiator. On a wall in the old city of Pompeii are the words 'Crescens the fighter holds the hearts of all the girls.'

Like chariot-drivers, successful gladiators could make money and, after some years, were given their freedom. Some were freed after a few fights because the crowd liked them. But some enjoyed the life and continued. Publius Ostorius was one of these men. He won fifty-one fights and became very famous.

● The show

Sometimes games lasted for many days. They were free because the emperor or other rich men paid for them. They started in the morning. At first, men fought against animals. Then at lunchtime criminals and, later, Christians were killed by animals. Many Romans did not stay for this, but some did.

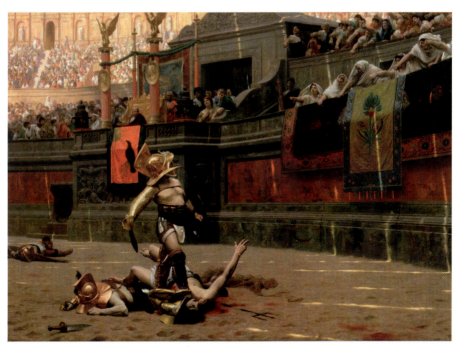

Pollice verso

After lunch the more serious activities began. The gladiators walked into and around the arena while musicians played. They then greeted the most important person there, and the fighting pairs were chosen. After a fight, the winner was given gold or silver. The losers could ask the emperor for their lives. Usually, he asked the crowd to decide and the people made signs with their thumbs. They probably did not point their thumbs down to ask for a gladiator's death. This idea comes mainly from the painting *Pollice verso* ('with turned thumb') by Jean Leon Gerome, and it was then used in many films. The sign for life was possibly closed fingers around the thumb – like a sword in its case. The sign for death was perhaps a movement of the thumbs like a moving sword. Nobody is sure.

● The end of the games

The games continued for hundreds of years. The number of holidays grew until, for the poor and unemployed, almost half the year was a holiday. Tens of thousands of men, women and animals were killed in the arenas. In 107 AD the games continued for 117 days. 4,941 pairs of gladiators fought and 11,000 animals died.

When Caligula was emperor (37–41 AD), some politicians and upper-class men had to fight in the Colosseum. The emperor Commodus (180–192 AD) also loved the games. In fact, he became a gladiator too, and fought in the Colosseum. Of course, the other gladiators' swords were not sharp. Commodus also killed animals, but not dangerous ones.

The Romans built arenas for gladiators all over the empire. Today you can find them from Portugal to Turkey and from Libya to Britain. But slowly, as Christianity became more popular, people stopped going to watch gladiators. The emperor Constantine tried to stop the games in 325 AD, but they were sometimes held after this, in Rome and in other places. When gladiators stopped fighting other gladiators, they continued to fight animals. Then in about 450 AD the games stopped completely.

Why did Romans enjoy the games so much? At first, gladiator fights followed the deaths of rich people, but the games were always about death. Many Romans died young. When people were asked to fight for the empire, they did. At the games, gladiators used their fighting skill to win. Or they died without a word. Criminals understood Roman law. Even wild animals were ruled by Rome. The games taught people about life and death, the Roman way.

CHAPTER 8

Republic to Empire

He talked to his friends and thought for a long time. Then he made a decision. 'The game has started,' he said, and he walked quickly across the bridge.

● Julius Caesar

Gnaeus Pompeius Magnus, or 'Pompey', and Marcus Licinius Crassus were politicians in Rome in 59 BC. Pompey was a general, and a very good one. The people of Rome liked him. Crassus was the richest man in Rome. He helped many politicians and they were grateful. The two men were very different, and each man hated the other.

At first, Julius Caesar was close to both men. His daughter was married to Pompey, and Crassus was a friend. Pompey and Crassus were able to work together with Caesar and the three men ruled Rome. When his time as a politician ended, Caesar was sent to the south of France. He fought there, and after seven years the country was under Roman rule. Caesar took his soldiers to Britain, too, but had to return to trouble in France.

Caesar's daughter died in 54 BC, so Pompey was then not a relative. Caesar worried about this. He thought that Pompey was a danger to him. The following year Crassus was killed in a war in Turkey. Then in 50 BC, the Senate ordered Caesar to leave his legions in France and return to Rome.

In the north-east of Italy, a small river meets the sea 15 kilometres north of Rimini. Its name was the Rubicon. Today, it is not at all important. The land on both sides of it is part of Italy. But in Caesar's time, only the south side was Italy. To the north was a part of the empire called Cisalpine Gaul.

In 49 BC, Caesar stood on the north side of this river. With him were the men of the 13th Legion. In front of Caesar there was a bridge, and the road to Rome. It was against the law for a general to take a legion into Italy. But without his soldiers, Caesar was afraid of Pompey. He talked to his friends and thought for a long time. Then he made a decision. 'The game has started,' he said, and he walked quickly across the bridge.

Caesar moved towards Rome with the 13th Legion behind him. There were other legions in Italy. Some joined Caesar. Others did nothing to stop him. The soldiers either liked Caesar or they were afraid of him.

Pompey feared for his life and left Rome. Caesar ordered more legions to come to Italy. They followed him south. Pompey quickly took a ship to Greece. But his legions were in Spain. Caesar decided to fight them there, so he took his men to Spain. He defeated Pompey's legions, and followed Pompey to Greece.

Death of Julius Caesar

Pompey's army was much bigger, but it was defeated by Caesar's men. Pompey escaped again, and this time he went to Egypt. Caesar returned to Rome and formed a new Senate from his own friends. This was the end of the Roman Republic.

● Cleopatra

When Pompey arrived in Egypt, he was murdered by soldiers of the ten-year-old king, Ptolemy XIII. Ptolemy was fighting his older sister, Cleopatra, and wanted Caesar's help against her. Egypt was not part of the Roman empire then, but Caesar wanted it and he went to Egypt. But he did not like Ptolemy, so he asked Cleopatra to visit him. This was dangerous, because Ptolemy's men were watching. Cleopatra arrived at the palace in a small boat. She hid inside a large bag and her friends carried her in. Caesar was amused. He found that he liked the young woman. His preference was for Ptolemy and his sister to rule together. But the young king did not like this idea, so Ptolemy and Caesar went to war.

Ptolemy attacked Caesar's ships at sea between Italy and Egypt, so Caesar burned Ptolemy's ships at Alexandria. He defeated Ptolemy's army and the king was killed. Caesar then lived for some time with Cleopatra. She later had his son and named the boy Caesarion. But Caesarion never knew his father because Caesar had important business in Rome.

● Murder

Back in Rome, Caesar started to make changes. Work began on many new buildings. He introduced new laws. People in places outside Italy became citizens of Rome. Some even joined the Senate. Caesar was, in many ways, a good ruler, but he acted like a king and some people wanted to return to the old ways. Two of these were Marcus Brutus and Gaius Cassius. On 15 March 44 BC, Caesar went to speak to the Senate. Brutus, Cassius and some others attacked him. They used knives and Caesar died a terrible death with twenty-three deep cuts in his body.

Caesar's death was a great surprise to the people of Rome. Brutus and Cassius spoke to them in the Forum. Some agreed that Caesar was too strong. Many did not. Then Caesar's friend Mark Antony brought the dead body to the Forum. He showed it to the people and told them of Caesar's plans for after his death – private gardens for the city and money for each citizen. The people became angry with the killers and the killers left the city. For some time, Antony ruled Rome.

● Octavian and Antony

The next ruler of Rome was a relative of Caesar. His name was Gaius Octavius, but now we call him Octavian. He was with a Roman army in present-day Albania when Caesar died. His friends thought he was not safe. He should stay with the army. His family told him to return to Rome, but quietly. Octavian had a different plan. First he changed his name to Gaius Julius Caesar Octavianus – or simply

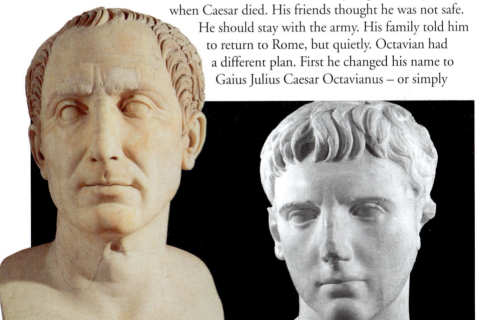

Julius Caesar and Octavian

'Caesar'. Then he crossed the Adriatic Sea to the south of Italy. A large number of soldiers were there. He spoke to them and many joined him. Octavian moved towards Rome. Old soldiers from Julius Caesar's legions lived along the way, and some also joined Octavian.

When Octavian arrived in Rome, Antony did not want to speak to him. Octavian was only eighteen, but Antony was a little worried by him. When Octavian tried to join the Senate, Antony stopped him.

Octavian left Rome. He went south again and about 10,000 of Julius Caesar's soldiers joined him. Two of Antony's legions also agreed to follow him. But Antony was more worried by Brutus. He took his other legions north and defeated him. Octavian followed Antony north. He fought Antony's army twice and won both times. Antony went to France and took more men from the Roman legions with him. But Octavian did not want another war between Roman soldiers. He returned to Rome and joined the Senate. Then he decided to talk to Antony. They met on an island in a river. Another man was there – Lepidus, a friend of Antony. The three of them agreed to rule together.

First, Antony and Octavian left Rome again to find Caesar's killers. The two armies fought at Philippi in Macedonia. Antony and Octavian's men won, and Brutus and Cassius later killed themselves.

● **Antony and Cleopatra**

Antony, Octavian and Lepidus each took a part of the Roman world. Lepidus got the west and went to live in Spain. Octavian had Italy, and Antony had

Antony and Cleopatra

the east. On his way to visit his new lands, Antony met Cleopatra at Tarsus in Turkey. The two became friendly and spent the winter together in Alexandria.

Lepidus took some legions to Sicily. Octavian thought that Lepidus was on his way to Rome. He found some men and moved towards him.

Lepidus' soldiers decided to join Octavian, and Lepidus gave up any hope of winning. He was sent by Octavian to a seaside town and told to stay there.

In Egypt, Cleopatra had two children with Antony. Octavian was not happy about this because his sister, Octavia, was Antony's wife. Antony also started a new government in Alexandria, and then he ended his marriage to Octavia.

Octavian was very angry and decided to go to war with Antony. He put a large army together and travelled to Greece. Antony's army moved north but the armies did not fight. Antony sailed to Egypt with his ships and fought Octavian's ships. After that, Antony and Cleopatra had to escape to Egypt, but Octavian followed with his army and Antony and Cleopatra killed themselves.

● The first emperor

Octavian was then ruler of the Roman world. The Senate gave him a new name, Augustus.

With the agreement of the Senate, Augustus made many changes. Nothing happened in Rome if Augustus did not want it. He was also careful never to make the rich people angry. He was, always, a very clever politician.

Augustus made changes to the army. He made life better for the soldiers, and then he sent them to wars far away from Rome, in countries like Germany. As a result, life became safer for ordinary people in the city. He also changed the way the government worked. There were no wars inside the empire, so life everywhere was less dangerous. People could make money. Because of this, they were happier with their rulers and began to accept the Roman way of life.

> **Roman names**
> Romans had a first name and a family name, and often another name was given to them later in their lives. Sometimes this came from their activities. The emperor Caligula's father was called Germanicus, for example, after he won a war in Germany. Sometimes it came from their looks. Julius Caesar's first name was Gaius; Julius was his family name and Caesar meant 'thick hair'. Sometimes names came from history. Caesar, Augustus, or both, were added to many later emperors' names.

Augustus changed the city of Rome too. He built the Forum of Augustus and many fine buildings. He died in 14 AD, more than forty years after he became the ruler of Rome and its empire.

Activities 5

5.1 Were you right?

Look back at your answers to Activity 4.4. Then write about:

1 two differences between the Colosseum and the Circus Maximus.

....
....
....
....

2 two similarities between the lives of gladiators and chariot drivers.

....
....
....
....

5.2 What more did you learn?

1 What were the jobs of these Romans? Put them into four pairs.

> Titus   Martial   Diocles   Juvenal
> Scorpus   Crescens   Vespasian   Publius Ostorius

writers: ....
emperors: ....
gladiators: ....
chariot drivers: ....

2 The men below fought on different sides. Which war happened first? Put the fights into the correct order, 1–5, and circle the names of the winners.

a ☐ Brutus / Antony
b ☐ Caesar / Ptolemy
c ☐ Octavian / Antony
d [1] Pompey / (Caesar)
e ☐ Antony and Octavian / Brutus and Cassius

The Romans

5.3 Language in use

Look at the sentence on the right. Then complete the sentences below with one of these words:

> Women fought as gladiators too, **until** this was stopped in 200 AD.

| after | as | before | when | while | until |

1 There was trouble in the street ....*after*......... a chariot team won a race.
2 Criminals fought wild animals .... they died.
3 .... they became more and more famous, drivers became richer.
4 Scorpus became rich .... he died.
5 .... important men sat at the front, ordinary Romans sat in higher seats.
6 Many Romans went home .... it was time for lunch.
7 Musicians played .... the gladiators walked into the arena.
8 There were more and more games .... almost half the year was a holiday.

5.4 What's next?

These were all built by the Romans. Match the names and the descriptions.

Vindolanda

1 the Pont du Gard   a an aqueduct in Rome
2 the Appian Way   b a large building in Rome
3 the Aqua Virgo   c a Roman camp in England
4 the Forum   d a Roman road
5 the Pantheon   e an aqueduct in France
6 Vindolanda   f the main square of Rome

CHAPTER 9

Roads and Water

People continued to use the roads for a long time after the empire ended. In fact, some are still in use today.

A Roman road

● Roman roads

In the Roman Forum, the main square of the city, there was a large stone. In golden letters it showed how far it was to different cities in the empire. All the roads of the empire started there, and new roads joined them. Every road went, sooner or later, to Rome.

The Appian Way was the first of the main roads. It is still the most famous. It was started in 312 BC on the orders of Appius Claudius Caecus, an important politician. It began in the Forum, and for the first 100 kilometres it was completely straight. A later road, the Via Aemilia, ran completely straight for 240 kilometres from Rimini to Piacenza.

Roman road-builders cut into the ground and took out earth and stones. They put down sand, then **concrete** with broken stone in it, then small stones. Onto the small stones they finally placed large stones which were flat on top. Roads were higher in the middle. The rain ran off them, along the side of the road and into holes in the ground. Usually, the road went down about half a metre into the ground, with another half-metre above it. But sometimes the Romans wanted higher roads. Perhaps the land was wet, or the soldiers

---

concrete /ˈkɒŋkriːt/ (n) something that is used to make floors, walls and roofs. When it dries, it is hard and usually grey.

needed to see around them. Some roads were as high as a metre and a half above the land.

For many hundreds of years, the roads worked very well. They helped the Roman army to move around. They also made business easier. Ideas, too, like Christianity, could travel quickly from one place to another.

People continued to use the roads for a long time after the empire ended. In fact, some are still in use today. And there were no better roads in this part of the world for more than a thousand years.

● Aqueducts

Built in about 19 BC, the Pont du Gard aqueduct is almost 50 kilometres long. It brought two hundred million litres a day of fresh water to the city of Nîmes in the south of France. It took 800–1,000 workers about five years to build. The aqueduct crosses the River Gardon on a bridge 275 metres long, built on top of two other bridges.

This was one of many aqueducts that the Romans built. People saw them as a sign of the strong rule of Rome, but they were able to drink the water and wash in it.

The first aqueduct for the city of Rome was completed in 313 BC and it brought water twelve kilometres into the city. In later years, as Rome grew, ten more aqueducts were built. The last was finished in 226 AD. The longest, the Anio Novus, was 87 kilometres long.

The Pont du Gard aqueduct

Above ground, aqueducts often look like bridges, but for most of their length they were just cut through rock. The water ran slowly downhill. One aqueduct continued underground all the way to Rome, but the builders usually wanted to bring the water into the city high above the ground. This meant that it could run downhill to different parts of the city. Because of this, for the last part of its journey, the water travelled on bridges.

Not all the water in an aqueduct came out of it at the other end. All along the way, landowners tried to steal some for their own use. In fact, sometimes none of the water reached Rome. When it did, the Romans also tried to steal it. Secret water pipes ran under the streets in many parts of the city. The water workers had to watch closely – but sometimes people gave them money and they looked the other way.

For hundreds of years an army of workers repaired the aqueducts and built new ones. When Rome was attacked in the last years of the empire, the aqueducts were cut one by one. Only the Aqua Virgo escaped because it was completely underground. One or two were later rebuilt and used for hundreds of years, but at that time most people had to get their water from the River Tiber. The river water was not clean and people became ill. The population fell from more than a million to about fifty thousand.

After the end of the empire, a thousand years passed before a new aqueduct was built in Rome. Today, three of the old Roman aqueducts still bring water to the city.

● A city of running water

When the water reached Rome, it ran through metal pipes to different parts of the city. Some was for the emperor and some was sold to rich citizens. They had pipes from the aqueducts to their houses. The rest was for ordinary people, but it only reached the ground floor. Most people had no water in their rooms. They took it from places in the street that were usually found about every hundred metres. But some parts of the city had no water at all for many years.

There were no toilets in most people's houses either. Some buildings had them on the ground floor for everyone who lived there. For a small payment people could also use toilets on the streets. Water ran through the better toilets all the time.

When the water left houses or street toilets, it ran along pipes under the street. But people sometimes emptied pots into the holes at the side of the streets that took rainwater away. The smell came back up into the streets and was often very bad in the summer. Rich people left the city and went to their farms.

CHAPTER 10

Writing, Counting and Building

'I have sent you socks and two pairs of shoes. Say hello to Elpis, Tetricus and all your friends. I hope that you all have good luck.'

● Writing

The Romans did not know about paper, but they made something similar from plants. For important writing they used the skins of young sheep. First, the skins were washed. Then they were pressed until they were flat and thin. Pens were made of wood or of metal. All the wooden pens have disappeared, but we still have some metal ones today.

For everyday writing, the Romans used **wax**. This came in a wooden box that opened like a book. When the writing was done, the box was closed. After the message was read, the wax was heated. Then it was used again.

Writing on wax

wax /wæks/ (n) something made from fat or oil. It is used to shine cars and furniture.

Hadrian's Wall

● Postcards

In the 1970s, historians were working at Vindolanda, a Roman camp in the north of England. It is just to the south of the wall that the emperor Hadrian built across the country. They found a large number of thin postcard-sized pieces of wood. Each of them is between one and three millimetres thick, and they have writing on them. When the message was written, the 'postcard' was closed like a book. In the north of the empire the Romans could not make any kind of paper from plants, so people used these pieces of wood.

When the Romans stopped using the camp, all the government messages were taken away. But messages between ordinary people were left behind. In fact, these are more interesting. They were written between 80 and 130 AD and tell us a lot about life on Hadrian's Wall. One of them, possibly from a Roman soldier's wife, says, 'I have sent you socks and two pairs of shoes. Say hello to Elpis, Tetricus and all your friends. I hope that you all have good luck.' In another one, an officer's wife invites another one to her birthday party.

The soldiers on Hadrian's Wall were not legionaries. They were paid half the money and did many of the simpler jobs. Most were German, but there were also men from other parts of Europe, from north Africa and the Middle East – and, as time passed, from Britain. But they all wrote in Latin. The postcards show us that many ordinary soldiers, and their wives, could read and write.

Chapter 10 – Writing, Counting and Building

● Counting

Today, we use nine different numbers, or ten if we think of zero as a number too. With these we can build all larger numbers. The number 50 is ten times bigger than 5, and 500 is ten times bigger than 50. Romans knew about the modern way of counting; it was used locally by people in many parts of the empire. But in our numbers, 15, with a one before the five, is larger than 5. In Roman numbers you make a number smaller when you put a one before it. V is five, but IV is four.

This difference made many sums difficult, but the Romans did not do sums with a pen. They either used a simple machine or a piece of wood with holes in it. In fact, the Romans were very like many people today. When they needed to do a sum, they used a machine.

The Greeks liked to study numbers, but the Romans did not. They wanted the answers to real problems. They used numbers to work out the size of buildings or roads, for example.

● Buildings

The Romans used concrete for new and different kinds of buildings. They could build to greater heights and they could cover larger areas with rounded roofs.

The Pantheon in Rome

Activities 6

6.1 Were you right?

Look again at Activity 5.4. Then match each name with another fact.

1. the Pont du Gard
2. the Appian Way
3. the Aqua Virgo
4. the Forum
5. the Pantheon
6. Vindolanda

a. It was straight for 100 kilometres.
b. 800–1,000 people worked on it.
c. It has a large rounded roof.
d. It is completely underground.
e. It is near Hadrian's Wall.
f. A stone was there, with golden letters.

6.2 What more did you learn?

1. Try these Roman sums. V is 5 and X is 10.

   a. IV + V = ...
   b. X − VI = ...
   c. III × II = ...
   d. X/V = ...

2. Complete these sentences.

   a. The Romans built with concrete mixed with ....
   b. Rain ran off Roman roads into ....
   c. Aqueducts carried ....
   d. When people used river water later, ...
   e. Water ran in pipes to ....
   f. Romans wrote on sheepskins with ....
   g. Everyday messages were written on ....

6.3 Language in use

Look at the sentence on the right. Then match the beginnings and endings of the sentences below. Write the letters, a–i.

> One or two **were** later **rebuilt** and **used** for hundreds of years.

1. ☐ Pens …
2. ☐ Some buildings …
3. ☐ The aqueducts …
4. ☐ When the writing …
5. ☐ The first aqueduct in Rome …
6. ☐ After a message was read, the wax …
7. ☐ Some piped water …
8. ☐ As Rome grew, more aqueducts …
9. ☐ A thousand years passed before a new aqueduct …

a were made of stone but this was unusual.
b was finished, the box was closed.
c were made of wood or of metal.
d was completed in 313 BC.
e were cut through rock.
f was sold to rich citizens.
g was built in Rome.
h was heated.
i were built.

6.4 What's next?

What do you know – or what can you guess – about these Roman emperors? Are these sentences true (✓) or not (✗)?

TIBERIUS
a ☐ He killed all his close relatives.
b ☐ He got tired of Rome and went to live on a small island.

CALIGULA
c ☐ He sometimes dressed as a woman.
d ☐ His horse had its own house with slaves and furniture.

CLAUDIUS
e ☐ He tried to burn Rome.
f ☐ He killed his third wife and his fourth wife killed him.

NERO
g ☐ He killed his mother and his second wife.
h ☐ He drove in chariot races and enjoyed acting.

CHAPTER 11

The Early Emperors

All through the time of the empire, Rome never found a way to choose a good emperor.

● Tiberius

Augustus, the first emperor, was worried about a war between Romans after his death, so he wanted his younger relative, Tiberius, to take his place. The Senate agreed. When Augustus died in 14 AD, Tiberius became the next emperor. But it seemed that Tiberius did not like the job very much. He gave a lot of the work to his son Drusus, and later to his friend Sejanus. This was not a success.

Sejanus used many spies. They watched rich citizens and listened to their conversations. When they said something against Tiberius, they were taken to court. Usually, after this, they were killed and Sejanus took their money.

In 26 AD Tiberius gave up his job completely. He left Rome and went to live on the island of Capri. Sejanus became stronger and stronger. Only he could speak to Tiberius and he almost became emperor. But then Tiberius began to fear Sejanus. He wrote to the Senate and asked them to stop him. They did this quickly and easily – they killed him. Tiberius stayed on Capri and became more and more crazy. Many people in Rome were killed on his orders. But in other parts of the empire, there was no war. The new ideas of Augustus worked well and life for ordinary people got better.

● Caligula

Caligula was born Gaius Julius Caesar Germanicus. His father was Augustus' grandson, Germanicus, a Roman general. When Caligula was very young, his father was fighting in Germany. The young boy spent time with the army, and he dressed like a small soldier. The soldiers liked him and called him Caligula. That meant 'little army shoes'.

He did not have a happy time as a child. Many people wanted to be the next emperor and there was fighting between them. Caligula's father then died mysteriously in Antioch, in modern Turkey. His mother was angry and returned to Rome. She called Sejanus a murderer. Caligula was sent away to live with relatives. They had little time for the boy and he was very lonely. His only friends were his three sisters.

Caligula's life was always in danger from Tiberius and Sejanus. Tiberius sent Caligula's mother to a small island. There, she died. Nobody is sure if she died naturally. Caligula's two oldest brothers, Nero and Drusus, were killed at this time. But then Tiberius asked the boy to go and live with him on Capri. Life there was very strange but Caligula enjoyed it. He liked to hurt slaves and watch gladiators fight and die. Tiberius did not try to stop him.

When Tiberius died – or, perhaps, was murdered – in 37 AD, Caligula became emperor. At first, he was a good emperor and the people liked him. He stopped the murders in Rome, gave money to his guards and paid for shows. He was the son of the popular general Germanicus and, unlike Tiberius, he was a relative of Julius Caesar.

But after a few months, Caligula fell ill. When he got better, he started acting strangely. He began to enjoy a very expensive lifestyle, and in a few months he spent all his money. He took more and more money from the citizens, but this was never enough. He killed rich people and took their land and money. He also fought with the Senate. He sent the most important politicians away and put new ones in their place. In fact, he was not very nice to politicians. Some had to run behind his chariot until they could not run any farther.

Caligula decided to take the army to Britain, but on the coast of France he changed his mind. He told his soldiers to take things from the beach. These showed their defeat of the sea. He liked to wear unusual clothes, or to dress as a woman. He ordered the deaths of his enemies and his friends. He gave very large and expensive parties. He also gave presents to his horse, Incitatus. In fact, the horse had its own house, slaves and furniture.

In 41 AD, after only four years as emperor, he was murdered by his guards. This was usually the only way to stop a bad emperor. Caligula was the first of many who died in this way.

Caligula

🟢 Claudius

Immediately after the murder, one of the guards was walking through the palace. He found a man who was hiding. This was Claudius, an uncle of Caligula and a grandson of Mark Antony. He was frightened because the guards were killing a lot of people that day. But they did not kill him. In fact, the next day they made him emperor.

Claudius had many problems. He was ill as a child, and after this he could not speak well. Also, his knees were weak, so he often fell down. But when he became emperor, he was suddenly much better. Perhaps, under Caligula, he tried to look ill so he did not look dangerous. His parents also kept him hidden as much as possible, and he spent the time with books. So he knew a lot of history and wrote about it. He was an intelligent man but not always pleasant. When he became angry with people, he often killed them.

Claudius was never in the army. But soon after he became emperor, he decided to become a great soldier too. He looked for a place to attack and he chose Britain. In a way, Britain was unfinished business: Julius Caesar's visits to Britain in 55 and 54 BC were short.

Claudius' plan probably was not a good idea. The Romans already received money from the country and the British were no danger to them. But in 43 AD, Claudius' general, Plautius, landed on the south coast with four legions. He fought his way north, and stopped at the River Thames. He waited there until Claudius arrived with more men eight weeks later. The army then built a bridge across the River Thames at a place that later became London. They crossed the bridge and there was no more fighting. Claudius continued to Colchester, the capital of the south-east. Sixteen days later, he left Plautius there and returned to Rome.

His rule made many things better in Rome. He changed the way people farmed. Also, food arrived more quickly from the countryside. He passed better laws for ordinary people. But his private life was less successful. He ended his first two marriages and killed his third wife. His fourth wife was Caligula's sister Agrippina. After some time he talked about ending this marriage too, but she was too quick for him. In 54 AD she **poisoned** his food and he died.

🟢 Nero

Nero was the son of Agrippina from her first marriage. He was mainly brought up by teachers and became interested in the theatre and music. Claudius thought of him as a son, and on his death Nero became emperor. He was seventeen at the time. It is possible that he helped to kill Claudius.

---

poison /ˈpɔɪzən/ (v) to kill someone by putting something in their food or drink

Chapter 11 – The Early Emperors

Nero

Agrippina wanted to rule with Nero, and the first money from that time shows their heads side by side. But Nero's teachers and other people in the palace did not want a woman as emperor. They spoke to Nero and he started to worry about his mother. Agrippina began to think about Britannicus, Claudius' son, as emperor. Soon after this, Britannicus was poisoned at a dinner. Many people thought that Nero was the murderer.

Nero then tried to poison his mother. He tried three times, but she knew all about life and death in the palace and ate carefully. Then he weakened the roof above her bedroom, but it did not fall on her. Next, he sent her to sea. The boat fell to pieces, but Agrippina swam to land. When Nero sent soldiers to kill her, Agrippina uncovered her stomach. She told them to kill her in the place that her terrible son came from. They did as she asked.

Many people think of Nero at the Colosseum. In fact, he was not very interested in gladiators. He preferred chariot-racing and even sometimes drove in races. He also liked to act in plays. He often acted for hours and people had to stay and watch. Sometimes women had babies before he finished.

When he did not like someone, they were killed on his orders. He thought his popular wife Octavia was against him, for example. So she was murdered. One of his teachers was the famous writer and thinker, Seneca. He was killed too. One day his next wife, Poppaea, became angry because he was home late from the races. Nero kicked her to death.

In 64 AD a fire started in Rome. It burned for a week and destroyed a large part of the city. Nero cleared the ground and built a big palace, the Golden House, with its own lake. But he probably did not play music while Rome burned. In fact, he sent men to put out the fire. He then helped the people who were now homeless. As a result of the fire, he made new rules for building.

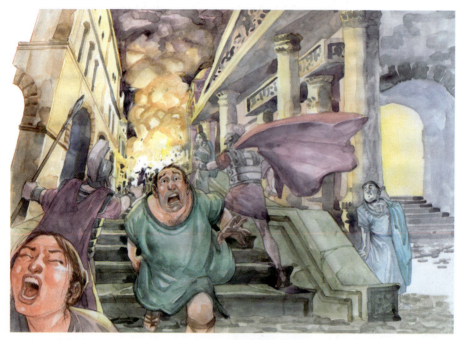

The fire of Rome, 64 AD

Fires in Rome were not unusual. But people believed that Nero started the fire. They thought he wanted the land for his palace. To stop that kind of talk, Nero pointed his finger at the Christians. He told his soldiers to find all the Christians in Rome. Some were burned alive in the gardens of the palace. Thousands of others were killed in other terrible ways.

Nero never visited his armies. He did not give them the usual present of money when he became emperor. He also ordered a popular general to kill himself. So he was not liked by the army. As time passed, the Roman people started to dislike him too. Finally, the Senate told him to leave Rome, and he ran away. He hid in a house near the walls of Rome. Nero killed many people in his life, but he could not kill himself. He ordered a slave to do it. His last words were, 'Now a great artist dies.'

All these four emperors – Tiberius, Caligula, Claudius and Nero – were relatives of Augustus, and of Julius Caesar before him. Three of them were very unpleasant men – historians are still not sure about Claudius. After Nero's death, the politicians were tired of that family. The next emperor, Galba, was not a great success either. Six months later, his guards killed him. All through the time of the empire, Rome never found a way to choose a good emperor.

CHAPTER 12

The Empire and After

Their ships were full of food for Rome, but the sea was stormy and they did not want to leave. Pompey said, 'It is necessary to sail. It is not necessary to live.'

● Becoming Roman

Under Tiberius, Caligula, Claudius and Nero (14–68 AD), life for relatives, politicians and rich Romans was often dangerous. But ordinary Romans did not worry about that. In fact, many of them enjoyed the bigger and bigger games at the Colosseum. And outside Rome, changes of emperor were not very important. Thanks to Augustus, the empire continued to work well. There was no war inside it and people did business and made money.

In different parts of the empire, local languages were spoken and local money was used. But everyone knew who the emperor was. And there was one language of government – Latin. Anyone – Syrian or Greek or Spaniard – could learn Latin and could enjoy the Roman way of life. Many men became citizens.

The Roman offer was a simple one. When people fought against them, the Romans did not just try to win. They tried to destroy their enemies. If they were not successful at first, they returned again and again. But when the enemy was defeated, the men could become Roman citizens. The Romans never worried much about nationality. Families on Rome's Palatine Hill with hundreds of years of Roman blood were seen as higher class, but under the law, a citizen was a citizen.

Julius Caesar invited men from other parts of the empire to join the Senate. Many Romans laughed at the foreigners. But this was the way Rome worked. They destroyed the enemy army, killed a few thousand people, and then talked to the rest. They explained the future of the people and showed them the good side of the Roman way of life.

● The beginning of the end

Not long after 400 AD, the empire in the west came to an end. The Huns had their own empire in the north of Europe, from Russia to Germany. Attila the Hun defeated the Romans in the Balkans, Greece and modern Turkey and took large areas of Roman land. In 451 AD he crossed the Rhine and occupied a number of cities. But he was stopped by a large Roman army at Chalons-sur-Marne, in France. We are told that more than 200,000 men died then. Attila went back across the River Rhine, but the following year he returned and attacked Italy.

He died soon after this, but the people in the north continued to attack. Others crossed from north Africa to attack Rome. Year after year it became more difficult for the Romans to fight them. People around the empire stopped thinking of Rome as the centre of the world. Then another group of people, the Goths, moved out of their lands in Romania and the Ukraine. In 410 AD they took Rome. They left, but in 455 AD it was taken again, by the Vandals from Germany. They were pushed back. The end came in 476 AD when the German chief Odoacer took Rome. Roman rule in the west ended. But the empire was not finished yet.

● West and east

For more than two hundred years after the death of Augustus in 14 AD, there was no war inside the empire. Then, in 235 AD, fighting started again. It continued for fifty years and during this time there were twenty-five different emperors. Almost all of them were either murdered or killed in wars. The trouble ended when Diocletian became emperor in 284 AD. He saw that the empire was too large. So he decided to cut it in two, on a north-south line between Italy and modern-day Albania.

When the Western Empire ended about two hundred years later, the Eastern Empire continued with its capital in Constantinople. The city took its name from the emperor Constantine in 330 AD. By his time, the east was safer than the west, so he made it his capital. He also made the city much larger and built a new protective wall.

Like Rome, Constantinople had seven hills. It also had an aqueduct, arenas for chariot-racing and gladiators, theatres and baths. In this city, the Roman way of life continued. For a long time it was the greatest city in the world. It was taken by the Turks in 1453. Then, under the name Istanbul, it became the capital of the Ottoman empire.

● How Rome changed the world

When the Roman empire ended, there was no more pay for the soldiers. Some went back to their own countries. Others stayed where they were. They found new work. This happened over many years and new people moved in and took their place. The map of Europe changed.

But many parts of the Roman way of life continued. One of these was Christianity. After Nero, the position of Christians slowly got better. Then Constantine became interested in the religion. While he was fighting near Rome in 307 AD, he saw a burning cross in the sky. As a result of this, he passed laws to protect Christians. Before he died, he also became a Christian. In 391 AD, under

Chapter 12 – The Empire and After

Important dates

BC

- 753 Romans believed the city began.
- 450 Roman laws were written.
- 313 The first aqueduct was built.
- 312 The Appian Way was started.
- 264–261 The first war with Carthage.
- 218–202 The second war with Carthage.
- 167 Polybius wrote about the Roman army.
- 149–146 The third war against Carthage.
- 110 Marius changed the Roman army.
- 90 People in other parts of Italy became Roman citizens.
- 73 Spartacus began the third slave war in Italy.
- 58 Julius Caesar began to fight in France.
- 55–54 Julius Caesar took the army to Britain.
- 49 Caesar led his soldiers into Rome.
- 46 Caesar changed the length of the year.
- 44 Caesar was murdered.
- 27 Octavian became emperor.
- 19 The Pont du Gard aqueduct was built.

AD

- 14 Octavian died. Tiberius became emperor.
- 26 Tiberius left Rome for Capri.
- 37 Tiberius died. Caligula became emperor.
- 41 Caligula was murdered. Claudius became emperor.
- 43 The Roman army entered Britain.
- 54 Claudius was murdered. Nero became emperor.
- 64 There was a large fire in Rome.
- 68 Nero died. Galba became emperor.
- 72 The Colosseum was started.
- 110–112 The Markets of Trajan were built.
- 122 Hadrian's Wall was started.
- 165 The Romans took Dura-Europos.
- 226 The last aqueduct was built.
- 257 The Romans left Dura-Europos.
- 285 The emperor Diocletian cut the empire in two: east and west.
- 306 The Baths of Diocletian were built.
- 313 The emperor Constantine passed laws to protect Christians.
- 330 Constaninople was named after Constantine.
- 337 Constantine became a Christian before he died.
- 339 Christianity became the main religion of the empire.
- 410 Rome was taken by the Goths.
- 451 Attila crossed the Rhine.
- 455 Rome was taken by the Vandals.
- 476 Odoacer took Rome. This was the end of the western empire.
- 534 The eastern emperor Justinian rewrote Roman law.

Theodosius I, Christianity became the main religion of the empire. Today, the Roman Catholic Church is one of the world's largest religions. Its centre is the Vatican City in Rome.

Another form of Christianity, Orthodox Christianity, grew in Constantinople. Today, this is the main religion of Greece, Bulgaria, Russia, Romania, Serbia, the Ukraine and other countries.

Roman laws were first written down in 450 BC. Twelve metal plates were put up in the Forum for everyone to see. Some laws did not continue for long. One of them stopped marriage between upper- and lower-class people. This was changed about five years later. But some laws were still in use at the end of the Western Empire, eight hundred years after this.

As the empire grew, the law grew too. It changed and took in new ideas. It tried to be fair to all citizens. It was written down, but judges could make their own decisions in special cases. In 534 AD, under the emperor Justinian in Constantinople, the law was rewritten in four parts. These were the emperors' laws, the greatest decisions of judges, information for students in law schools and new laws of Justinian. Today, the law in many countries comes from Roman law.

From Latin came French, Italian, Spanish, Catalan and other languages. Latin was also the international language of Europe for hundreds of years. It was used in Roman Catholic churches until the 1960s. Latin words passed into English through religion, and also through the language of law, government and medicine.

In 46 BC Julius Caesar changed the number of days in Roman months. The year was too long because so many days were added for religious reasons. To correct this, he made the next year 445 days long. Then on January 1 of the year after that, a year of 365 days came in, with 366 days in every fourth year. In 1582 Pope Gregory XIII made a small change, but we use the Julian months today. One month, July, is named after him, and another is named after the emperor Augustus.

● **People of Rome**

Many people do not think of the Romans as very pleasant or interesting people. Their empire was built on slavery and many of the slaves were hurt or killed. When Romans occupied a new land, they often killed thousands of people. And at the Colosseum and other arenas across the empire, they enjoyed watching men and animals die. The Romans had very few new ideas; most of their ideas came from the Greeks. But unlike the Greeks, their thinking had a clear purpose.

Chapter 12 – The Empire and After

The Roman forum today

Roman paintings were good, but not wonderful. Their literature was also good, but writers were not very important to them. But Romans worked hard and were very brave. And they always believed that they could do the job.

One story shows this well. The great general Pompey spoke to some Roman sailors. Their ships were full of food for Rome, but the sea was stormy and they did not want to leave. Pompey said, 'It is necessary to sail. It is not necessary to live.' So they sailed.

This was the Roman way. Time after time they put their city before their own lives – and they changed the world.

Talk about it

1 Work in groups of three or four.

> It is January 10, 49 BC. The Senate has told Julius Caesar to return to Rome. Now he is on the north side of the River Rubicon. He has the 13th Legion with him. But it is against the law for him to take them into the real Italy on the other side of the river. Caesar has to make a decision.
>
> ● He can refuse to return to Rome but he will become less important. The 13th Legion may stay with him for some time, but sooner or later the Senate will take them away.
>
> ● He can go to Rome without his soldiers. He may be safe if he does this, but Pompey may try to kill him.
>
> ● He can take the 13th Legion to Rome. If they are not defeated, he can rule in Rome. But this will end the Roman republic.

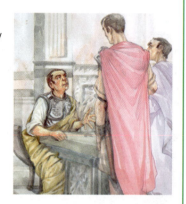

Student A: You are Julius Caesar. Ask your friends what you should do.

Students B–D: You are Caesar's friends. What should he do? Help him to make a decision.

2 Work in pairs.

a Talk about your own country's past and make notes. Was it ever part of an empire? If not, why not? If it was, which empire was it part of? When? For how long? What signs are there now of the occupation?

Notes

b Use your notes to give a short talk to another pair of students. Answer questions.

Write about it

1 Work in pairs. Imagine that you live in a country that was part of the Roman Empire. You are going to write an article about Roman successes for a student magazine.

Discuss what you are going to write about. You can choose one or more of these subjects: water, buildings, law, arenas, government, religion, the Latin language. You can also choose a different subject if you have the information.

2 Now write the article and find a picture for it.

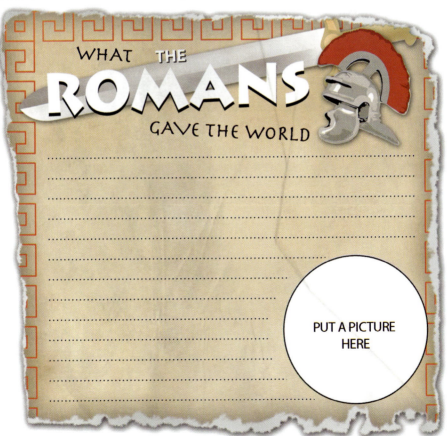

WHAT THE ROMANS GAVE THE WORLD

PUT A PICTURE HERE

Project *A Roman Dinner Party*

1 Work in pairs. Use books or the Internet to find information.

Imagine that you live in Rome. You are invited to dinner at a rich friend's house. What will you find there and what will happen? What kind of furniture will there be? How will you eat? What kind of food will there be? Which other people will be there? What will you do during and after the meal? Make notes.

Notes

2 Work in groups of six to eight people. You are all going to be at the same dinner party.

You are going to discuss the fact that the empire – and the number of citizens – continues to grow. Look at the next page. Decide who is going to play the part of each person. Then work alone. What do you want to say about the subject for discussion? Write notes on your opinions and your reasons for them.

Notes

Project A Roman Dinner Party

A You are a rich Roman. This is your house and your dinner party. You want to be a politician and you have very strong opinions about everything. It is your job to start the conversation. You also want to keep your guests happy.

B You are the wife of the head of the house. You want your comfortable life to continue, and you want more cheap slaves to help you in the house.

C You are the son of the house, a young adult. You have little interest in life outside Rome. You don't work because you can't find a job. You don't want to work with your father or his friends, or continue taking his money.

D You are the daughter of the house, a young adult. Your husband is a legionary and you haven't seen him for two years. You want a baby.

E You are a guest. You are a very famous gladiator from another part of the empire. You are still a slave, but soon you are going to buy your freedom.

F You are a guest. You were an army general and you are now a successful politician. You help to decide where the army should go. It is getting difficult to find new soldiers to occupy new lands.

G You are a guest. You are a very successful businessman from another part of the empire. You travel a lot, looking for new and interesting things. Then you buy and sell them.

H You are a guest. You are from another part of the empire and you are a local politician. You are not happy about the changes to the way of life in your area.

Continue to work in your groups.

Pull your desks together and sit around them. Imagine that you are now at the dinner party. Discuss the subject of the growing empire and give your opinions. The head of the house should start the conversation.

Project *A Roman Dinner Party*

4 **You are still the person whose part you played at the dinner party.**
You have listened to other opinions, and have probably added ideas to your own. Write a letter to a local newspaper. What do you think about the fact that the empire, and the number of citizens, continues to grow? What should the government do? Tell readers of the paper.